P9-DVD-029

Prayers for Puppies,
Aging Autos,
and Sleepless Nights

# Prayers for Puppies, Aging Autos, and Sleepless Nights

—— God Listens to It All ——

## Robert Jones

### Illustrations by Gay Guidotti

Westminster/John Knox Press
Louisville, Kentucky

© 1990 Robert Jones

*All rights reserved.* No part of this book may be reproduced or transmitted in any form or by any means, electronic or mechanical, including photocopying, recording, or by any information storage or retrieval system, without permission in writing from the publisher. For information, address Westminster/John Knox Press, 100 Witherspoon Street, Louisville, Kentucky 40202-1396.

Originally published in 1990 by Vistabooks as *Prayers for Puppies and Other Creatures and Things.*

*Book design by Drew Stevens*

Published by Westminster/John Knox Press
Louisville, Kentucky

This book is printed on acid-free paper that meets the American National Standards Institute Z39.48 standard. ∞

PRINTED IN THE UNITED STATES OF AMERICA
9   8   7   6   5   4   3   2

**Library of Congress Cataloging-in-Publication Data**

Jones, Robert.
   [Prayers for puppies and other creatures and things]
   Prayers for puppies, beat–up autos, and sleepless nights /  Robert Jones ; drawings by Gay Guidotti.
        p.      cm.
   Originally published: Prayers for puppies and other creatures and things. S.1. : Vistabooks, 1990.
   ISBN 0-664-25356-3 (acid–free paper)

   1. Prayers.   2. Meditations.   3. Christian poetry, American.
I. Title.
BV260.J68   1993
242'.8—dc20                                        92-40902

Dedicated to the people
of the Guerneville Community Church
and the Monte Rio Community Church
and their friends and neighbors

# CONTENTS

| | |
|---|---:|
| Prayer for Puppies | 11 |
| Prayer for Going on a Diet | 13 |
| Prayer for a Stray Cat | 15 |
| Prayer for a Dead Duck | 17 |
| Prayer for a Sleepless Night | 19 |
| Prayer for Super Sunday | 21 |
| Prayer for Pancakes | 23 |
| Prayer for a Party | 24 |
| Prayer for the Morning After | 25 |
| Prayer in a Desert | 27 |
| Prayer for a Three-Foot Putt | 29 |
| Prayer for a Cough | 31 |
| Prayer for a Middle-Aged Body | 32 |
| Prayer for Popcorn | 35 |
| Prayer Upon Losing a Job | 37 |
| Prayer for Rendering to the IRS | 39 |
| Prayer for a Meteorite | 41 |
| Prayer for the Blahs | 43 |
| Prayer in October | 45 |
| Prayer for a Class Reunion | 47 |
| Prayer in a Crowd | 49 |
| Prayer for Socks | 51 |
| Prayer During a Divorce | 52 |
| Prayer Out of Boredom | 55 |
| Prayer for a Redwood Tree | 57 |
| Prayer of the Ordinary | 59 |
| Prayer in Traffic | 61 |
| Prayer for Blackberries | 63 |
| Prayer on a Visit to a Dying Friend | 65 |
| Prayer at a School Board Meeting | 66 |
| Prayer for Purposes | 69 |
| Prayer for Safe Travel | 71 |
| Prayer in the Morning | 73 |
| Prayer About Inconsistencies | 75 |

Prayer for a Beat-Up Car 77

Prayer in April 79

Prayer for a Vegetable Garden 81

Prayer for Gazing 83

Prayer for Jazz 85

Prayer for Whales 87

Prayer for a Mountain 89

Prayer for a Christmas Cat 91

Prayer for a Dream 93

Prayer for a Prayer 94

Quench not the spirit.

In every thing give thanks.

Pray without ceasing.

*—St. Paul's First Letter to the Thessalonians*

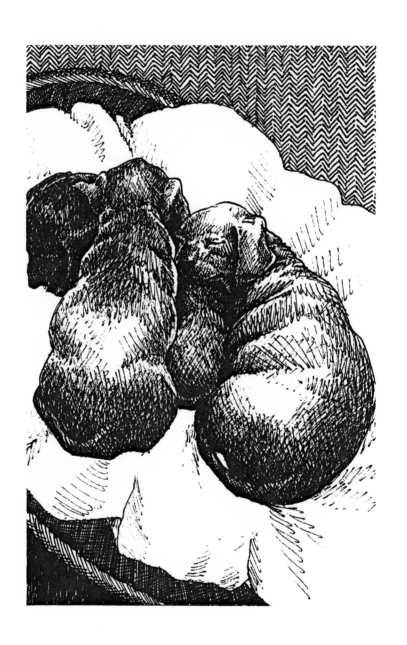

# PRAYER FOR PUPPIES

Maker of the animals,
we pray today for little pups.
We praise you
that even their blindness and whining
are ways of happiness in this world.

May they never be alone and cold.
May their wishes for a friendly home
be speedily fulfilled.
And spare them please all curiosity
for fast-moving machines.

Help us to see in these spots on our rug
little tokens of that baptism
into a new and special life
shared only with a dog.

And teach us forgiveness
through countless ruined shoes
and other chewings.

In this fluffy gift,
grant us glimpses of that inheritance
reserved especially for the meek,
gladden our hearts
with the licks and wiggles
of spontaneous love,
and teach us the meaning of sniffs,
scratches, and wagging tails.

We lift this bit of life before you
and ask you to deliver us now
from ringworm, fleas,
and cats that won't scare.

# PRAYER FOR GOING ON A DIET

Beginner of everything, help me to get started.
I am sore afraid of failing.
I am a coward in the face of minor pain.
I am dangerously close to believing
that procrastination is my nature,
dangerously close to blaming my weakness on you.

Compel me, please,
between the grapefruit and the celery,
to do what I must do.
Drive my thoughts away from poundage.
Make calories something less
than my ultimate concern.

Fit slimness in as part of my life,
one goal among the many you help me achieve.
Oh, may there come a day
when I praise you for cottage cheese.

Now curb my jealousy of those
who can eat and drink and still be merry.
Unquicken my lust for a plate piled sinfully high.
And remind me, always, that half your children
feel a hunger more fierce than mine.

# PRAYER FOR A STRAY CAT

God of the loners,
God of those who survive,
be with this black and white cat
that everyone in the neighborhood calls "ours"
but by her own choice is nobody's.

Sometimes she's gone for weeks
and there's no way to know she's come back
except for paw prints across the hood of the car.

She is aloof and self-sufficient,
sure of her worth,
a beautiful cat living a hard life
that she is unwilling to trade for any other.
Not one of us has offered her a saucer of milk,
and yet she appears not to feel slighted.

So far as I know, she doesn't have a name,
but she has this presence among us
of tameness bordering on the wild,
of tarnished grandeur,
of knowledge we haven't learned yet
or have forgotten long ago.

There is something old and young about this cat,
something eternal and flighty,
something we can wonder about
but will never fully perceive.

Last night she slept in grasses or thickets
or under a rotting porch.
This morning she sits on the woodpile
eyeing a bird.

She pounces and feathers fly,
and she sidles off victoriously,
the limp bird in her mouth,
to enjoy what you have graciously provided
in the ferocious harmonies of this world.

# PRAYER FOR A DEAD DUCK

Bestower of wisdom,
have special care for what we call dumb animals,
for Dougie the Duck was certainly one of them.
He was a duck who wanted to be a dog.

He chased cars, and when he caught one
he pecked at the rolling tires
and quacked outrageously with a quack
that tried to sound like a bark.

The other day he chased a car
and caught it just as it swerved,
and it squashed him flat.
Now we are sad,
and our children are sad,
and the older people in our neighborhood
are especially sad.

Dougie was the life of our little party here
on this shady bend of the road.
He was a character among us,
obviously weird, but lovable,
and he helped us know that our own weirdness
is part of loving and being loved.

We ask you to receive him
and to grant eternal rest
to Dougie's ducky-doggie soul,
assuming such creatures have souls,
which seems like a safe assumption
given the way Dougie was.

As you must know,
in trying to be what he wasn't,
Dougie was a lot like us.

# PRAYER FOR A SLEEPLESS NIGHT

Keeper of the people,
who neither slumbers nor sleeps,
I am with you tonight.

My mind is a racetrack of useless ideas.
My hands are sweaty.
My feet drop off with cold.

Help me forget whatever it is
I'm trying to remember.
Help me believe that these images
swirling in the darkness
are not from you.

Notice, I have not asked for sleep,
for that is as near as the pillbox or the toddy.

Rather, bring now a truer perception
of dimness, shadow, and quiet.
Lessen my need to be always in control.
Banish my fear of where this hour may lead me,
and lift me above the petty discomforts
of flattened pillow and wrinkled sheets.

O God of rest and gladness,
teach me acceptable ways through schedules
that go against my plans,
and stay my faith in relaxation,
which comes as surely as the dawn.

# PRAYER FOR SUPER SUNDAY

Today, O God,
you who hurled the universe into space
and set the planets spinning in their flight
will be eclipsed by padded, helmeted gods
who at best can throw a football eighty yards.

Amid the superlatives of this hour—
the miraculous catches,
the brilliant passes,
the perfectly timed leaps—
remind us that you are above all and beyond all
and that any excellence in our doings
is because you are in all and through all as well.

May the violence and the strutting
be left behind when the game is over.
May we allow music and pageantry to stir us
in a multitude of more subtle ways.
May loyalty and courage remain
even when the context is more than a game.

Guard us from the easy notion
that these activities are what the Sabbath is for.
Move us beyond our simple judgments
about what is glorious and great.
Subdue our dreams of an eternally reserved
fifty-yard-line seat.

And finally, when the cheering is over
and the stadium empties
and darkness falls once more,
be pleased to reveal in us a way of greatness
that does not require another's hurt.

# PRAYER FOR PANCAKES

God of all goodness,
I thank you for these pancakes
steaming on the table.
I thank you for the butter and the syrup
running to the edge of my plate,
though the butter is corn oil margarine
because of my high cholesterol.

This is how breakfast should be.
It reminds me of my mother,
who on special days made Bisquick pancakes,
cracking in extra eggs
before whipping the batter
with a long-handled spoon.

She ladled the pancakes onto a griddle
placed over two burners on the gas stove.
When I got big enough she let me flip them.
I had to wait until they bubbled;
then I turned them over
and listened to them hiss
and saw them rise.

I make these pancakes the same way she did
except I scoop out the egg yolks
and do my cooking in a pan.

And I eat these pancakes now
and notice they are not the same as hers.
I sip fresh coffee and think of my mother,
of how crisp the edges of her pancakes were,
and, in the middle, how thick and golden brown.

## PRAYER FOR A PARTY

Lord of the dance, the feast,
the very special wine,
this should be some party.
Help us not to mess it up
by straining for more fun
than we can stand.

May we say some sensible things
even in hilarity.
May the flirting stay
within the bounds of propriety.
May the children sleep soundly
while we are gone.

Once I get this last look in the mirror,
let me give no thought to my appearance.
As only you can, scatter my self-consciousness
and bring to nothing all my efforts
to seem more than I am.

Now bestow upon us that freedom
to riotously overindulge
for which your followers are noted.
And, in the fullness of your time
be pleased to grant us
a story, a toast, or a song
that will strengthen our circle of friends.

Finally, please remind me,
for the sake of all I hold dear,
to dance the last dance with my wife
and let her drive home.

# PRAYER FOR THE MORNING AFTER

O God of justice and mercy,
this just isn't fair.
Only your worst enemy should suffer
the pangs that pang me.

A decrepit, wounded wretch
has housed himself in my body.
My eyes are open sores
tortured with grainy light.
My head is being blasted
from one sand trap to another.
My tongue is a slab of rancid butter.

Bless me now with aspirin
and gentle anti-acid fizzes.
Anoint my head with bags
of slowly melting ice.
And deliver me, I implore,
from wry smiles, shaking heads,
and slightly smirking faces.

Strike dumb all those
who speak above a whisper.
Afflict with palsy
anyone who tries to fix me an egg.
And through this rueful morning,
send my precious children anywhere
but near this bed of pain.

I know I must rise at last
and own this terror as my doing.
But for now, be pleased to visit those
who toasted with me and urged me on
with heads as big as mine.

## PRAYER IN A DESERT

God of emptiness and shadows,
this land is vast and mysterious,
eerie in fading light.

The road through here,
though straight ahead for miles,
seems aimless and wandering.

I drive toward the setting sun,
jagged mountains to the north of me,
peaks without names so far as I know,
valleys hidden by the growing dark.

The yucca, the ironwood, the Joshua trees
show signs of constant struggle.
Strong and terribly fragile,
they grow where I could not survive.

Help me remember how you were with your people
as they wandered in a wilderness.
Help me find your guiding cloud and fire.
Help me accept the worth of environments
hostile to my needs.

Jesus was tempted in the desert, we are told,
and later went there to pray.
May I have courage to enter empty places
and be taught by what is frightening and holy.

May I be at peace where no one else is,
where the animals live in holes underground,
where the smallest flower seems like a miracle,
where bushes sometimes burn with dazzling light.

# PRAYER FOR A THREE-FOOT PUTT

O God of space and time,
of matter and velocity,
this little dimpled ball
with Titleist written on it
sits but a yard away from a par
on the eighteenth hole.

I realize there are floods and fires
and famines on the earth
and terrible weathers
and huge imponderable outcomes
to which you must attend,
but in the midst of spinning worlds
and your far-flung actions,
let me tell you something
of what is going on right here.

After a decent drive
and a wobbly two-iron
across the freshwater marsh,
my ball landed in the sand.
I blasted out to this sloping green
just three feet from a four.

The grass is smooth,
the wind has died,
the sun is warm upon my back.
Gentle waves are lapping at the shore.
It's a lovely afternoon
and I thank you for it,
but you have to know,
in twenty years of trying,
I've never parred this hole.
If I don't make this putt
I'll be miserable for a month.

Therefore, do what you can.
Steady my hands and arms and shoulders.
Plant my feet securely on your good earth.
Keep my head from moving,
and take away the feeling
that I have already missed.
The line is just inside the edge,
a little right to left.

This must be close to nothing
in the vastness of your care,
so please don't bother
more than you think you should.
But surely you understand
that a par on a hole like this
would be a kind of spiritual triumph
for a struggling soul like me.
Not only that, I'd win the skin
and halve two bets and a press.

# PRAYER FOR A COUGH

God of breath and spirit,
of polluted, I suppose, and unpolluted air,
there is something in my throat.
It itches. It tickles. It distracts my thoughts.
It disturbs me all the day long.

I have just gotten over a virus, they say,
and for that I am grateful.
But what about viruses in the first place, God?
Why must we have them
and all those other germs they say are there
but which we cannot see?

I didn't sleep last night or the night before.
I wheeze and gurgle throughout the day.
I swallow sticky-sweet syrups and bitter pills.
I cough until my ribs begin to ache.

You must know that when I'm coughing
I don't care about the homeless or world peace.
I don't care if the churches are full or empty.
All I want is a little relief.

And I am not grateful to be reminded
that a tiny vapor or speck of dust can undo me.
I am not thrilled to be mainly a spasm.
I am not happy to be convulsed.

Honestly, God, if this is your way
of telling me I'm a mere mortal,
I've had enough.

# PRAYER FOR A MIDDLE-AGED BODY

You hold all things together;
how come I am falling apart?

Yesterday my ankle was swollen.
Today my shoulder hurts.
For none of this is there any explanation.
I have not jogged nor hoed nor tried to chop wood.

My capacity for thought shrivels to nothing
right after dinner. Reading at night
is now a brief prelude to slumber.
If I watch TV, I can't make it through the movie,
let alone the bloody news.

You filled the earth with all kinds of foods,
but I can no longer eat them.
Shellfish causes my stomach to rumble.
Hot sauce burns my heart for three days.
I watch my salt, avoid red meats,
am especially careful of sugar and booze.
I will not mention the things that make me sneeze.

You who see into every corner,
can you know what it's like
to be fitted for trifocals?

You who hear every whisper, remember me
when I must ask people to repeat
whatever it is they've just said.

You whose arm is strong,
have pity as mine becomes weaker.

I yearn for the days
when I could run the track,
throw the ball, swim the lap,
work the fields,
and party all night long.

And I would like once again
to chase an idea through the darkness
into the breaking dawn.

O Perfect One,
deliver me from the fear of my imperfections.
Grant me some peace
about the limits of my capacity to endure.
Provide me with those challenges
my pounding heart and queasy gut can handle.
And help me praise you for the fleshly joys
that come in spite of cricky thumbs, fallen arches,
and this gray-streaked hair.

# PRAYER FOR POPCORN

God of the earth and its goodness,
this is one of the best things you do.
Well, you get some help from farmers
and poppers and salters and butterers,
but surely anything this wonderful
transcends human accomplishment.

Once again, I remember my mother:
how on Sunday nights she popped popcorn
in a long-handled wire basket
she shook upon a pie tin turned upside down
over a burner on the stove.

The first few pops were like miracles,
and then the rapid-fire popping started,
and then the aroma of earth and fields
and harvests and heaven filled the house.

Mother poured the popcorn into a huge yellow bowl,
dribbled on the butter she had melted
 in a small tin cup placed over the pilot light,
and sprinkled on just enough salt.

Then, with a knife in one hand
and nothing in the other,
she fluffed and caressed the popcorn,
spreading salt and butter evenly upon it
and sending more and more of the smell
of goodness and good times
into our nostrils and into our lives.

Praise to you, O God,
For Sunday night traditions
and this fresh-popped corn.

# PRAYER UPON LOSING A JOB

Creator, Sustainer, Creator Anew,
it is also true of me
that my work is mostly who I am.
I know myself in my qualifications.
I am alive when I am useful,
and this morning I have nothing to do.

Oh, I can pretend I'm on vacation.
I can head for the hills
with my sleeping bag and tent.
I can go to the movies.
I can play a little golf.

Or I can paint the screens
or dig in the garden
or prune the scraggly ivy
and gather the clippings into a pile
and take two hours for lunch
and nap all afternoon.
But none of this is fun
if you don't have a regular job.

O God, protect me from feeling I am absent.
Reduce the swell of discouragement
that rises and wrecks my day.
Have mercy, for I cannot be idle
and feel I am pleasing you.

Now take away my resentment
of carpenters, janitors, tailors, all at work,
and kids selling papers on the street.
End my jealousy of neighbors
who get into their cars
and head for the rotten commute.

Calm me as I read the morning paper
and come to the help wanted ads.
Steady my nerves
as I dial for appointments.
Control my rage
as I fill out ridiculous forms.
Comfort my grief
for my tiny cluttered office,
for the desk I deplored,
for my squeaky chair,
and the bothersome details of my former work.

Sooner rather than later, I pray,
help me to see this as a chance
to make a worthy change.
Give me a glimpse of who I am
apart from what I do.
And grant me a courage
I never thought I would need
to rise at a reasonable hour
and have a good breakfast and bathe.

# PRAYER FOR RENDERING TO THE IRS

You who made the ancients strong in battle,
steady now my damp and shaking hand.
To Caesar I would gladly render,
but the IRS causes me to tremble, tremble.

Good God, you know me for an honest soul.
Except for stealing pumpkins as a kid,
at which, in your great wisdom, I was caught,
and for which, in the wisdom of my father,
I dearly paid, I have cheated no one.
I never had a ticket fixed,
never argued with the bank on my account,
never drove the car-pool lane alone.
Why is it, then, I shudder to sign my name?

God, this exercise drains me.
I fear people I hope I'll never know.
I'm anxious now, and I can't help it,
but settle me down tomorrow,
for if life is more than death,
it's surely more than taxes,
and there is much good, I pray,
this money goes to do.

# PRAYER FOR A METEORITE

We call them falling stars, O God,
these heavenly sparks that catch us up
in a glimpse of arcing light
just before they are gone.

And tonight, this falling star
reminds me of my father
who worked six days a week in a department store
and on Sunday nights went outside to look at stars,
his eyes wide with wonder.
If one fell, he pointed silently
and made a long sweep with his arm.

One night, when the earth was passing through
the tail of a comet, and bright flashes
streaked the darkness in all directions,
a bunch of us kids ran through the streets
screaming and waving at the sky.

My father had gone up on the roof that night,
and he lit matches and threw them down
behind our house toward the clothesline.
It looked like falling stars
were hitting the ground in our backyard,
so we ran in a pack that direction.

Then we heard my father laugh,
and we saw the matches in his hands,
and we felt silly but also a little sad
that something so far away
had not come close to us.

# PRAYER FOR THE BLAHS

On the days my job is lousy
and I do a lousy job,
I need your help, O God,
and the assurance you are busy
doing, as always, your eternal best.

Such a day has just gone by.
My accomplishments are nil.
My plans for tomorrow lie unnoticed.
I stare at the garden wall
and watch the ivy grow upon it.

And now I confess my enjoyment of such days.
I acknowledge my need for them
in the midst of great wrongs to right,
hungry mouths to feed,
and these three letters that must be typed
and gotten in the mail.

Bless you for not needing me
to be energetic all the time.
Bless you for the sparkle of sun
through the branches of the poplar tree
that grows no matter what I do or do not do.
Bless you for clouds on the horizon
and the rising, murky river.

Speak to me and overcome my anxiousness
about this kind of day,
and help me notice whatever new intention
I may be turning to.

## PRAYER IN OCTOBER

Commander of early frosts and biting breezes,
the days swirl by swiftly now,
and I beg you to cause them to linger.
I relish these autumn blessings,
revealing as they do a calmer glory
than the dazzlements of spring.

And yet, O God, I often pause and wonder,
in these twilit afternoons,
about the years that pile like piling leaves,
like yellow piling leaves
against the walls and fences.

I wonder how anything is selected and remembered
from the red and golden woods of Pennsylvania,
from Kansas full of rusted corn,
from the ruddy poison oak
among the evergreens of California.

I wonder what thought or deed can stand, O God,
against your greenings and glowings,
what light prevails against the thickening dark.

A dull autumnal peace burrows in my soul,
and I am overwhelmed by a kinship
between beauty and dying.
Vague sadnesses descend
and condense on forest and plain.
I ache for the weather to change.

Teach me to behold this season
without fear or elation—
gust and cloud and raindrop,
the smell of the fallow earth,
the driven mist, the skin a-tingle,
the last red apple clinging to its tree—
and help me to be grateful
for the need to wear a sweater
and for my quickened pace against the chill.

Yes, help me to discover,
in the moods and shadows of October,
the deeper harvests of your turning world.

## PRAYER FOR A CLASS REUNION

God of all our years,
since last we were together
some of us have gotten sick and gotten well,
some of us have gotten sick and died,
and all of us have gotten older.

And all of us have done things
we wish we could do over.
All of us have said things
we wish we hadn't said.
And most of us have thought great thoughts
that didn't come to much.

Still, by and large
we did the best we could,
given who we are.
We helped and harmed.
We lived our lives.
We tried.

We thank you for the strength to keep on trying.
We thank you for the memories of this night.
And we thank you for these blessed name tags
that give us confidence to mingle
among old enemies and friends.

# PRAYER IN A CROWD

Savior of the multitudes,
this crowd frightens me.
I am pressed in by strangers.
I am shoved where I do not wish to go.
I feel like a splash in the river
or a tiny speck of sand.

God, is there room in the universe
for so many eternal destinies?
Are there hillsides enough for all our graves?
Is it possible you know my name?

So few of us are handsome or shapely.
Fewer still seem happy or wise.
And yet you tell us we are made
a little less than angels.
Right now that's hard to believe.

In the midst of all these people,
prayers seem useless and confusing,
so many desires rising to the sky,
so many pleadings to contradict mine.

I ask only that my two feet
be permitted to step on natural ground
and that I remember who I am
and where I want to go
as I am moved along
by the alien will of this crowd.

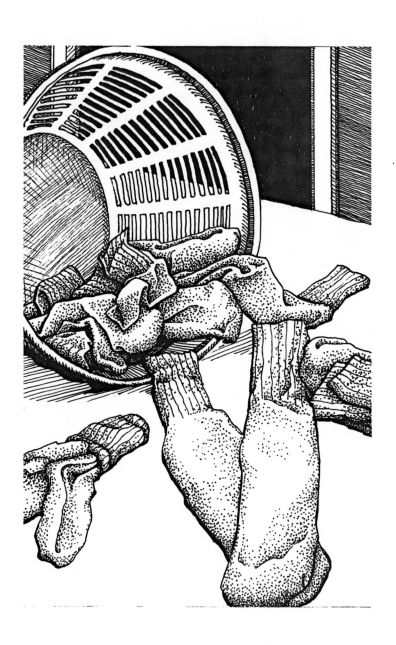

## PRAYER FOR SOCKS

Renewer of everything,
I want fresh socks.
I can already feel them on my feet,
warm and thick and fluffed by the dryer.

I want the cotton ones blended with wool,
extra thickness at heel and toe,
the elastic slightly unravelled,
the fibers a little bit loose.

No, I don't want new socks, so tight
you have to scrunch your foot into them
or else roll them up and then unroll them
in order to get them on.
I want socks that have been worn
but still have lots of bounce,
lots of warmth and comfort.

I see my socks tucked in their drawer.
They nudge each other and press together,
anxious, perhaps, to be the ones I choose.
They are brown or black or blue,
dark and purposeful, the way socks should be.

I pick the dark blue ones
with a thin gold stripe around the ankles,
my college colors.
I slip them on and finish dressing
and go forth into the day
convinced I am upheld and supported
by the good earth,
a good God,
and these fresh and wonderful socks.

# PRAYER DURING A DIVORCE

Joiner together,
we are putting asunder.
We know it's the right thing to do,
so why does it feel so wrong?

Just a few years ago, everything was wonderful,
or at least good enough to keep us going.
Now we fret, we chide, we compete.
We sit in silence daring the other to speak.

How did we drift apart?
Is the trouble as little as it seems?
Why can't I try any longer?
What about Christmas next year?

Upholder of justice,
I want my share of the records,
some candlesticks, and my favorite chair.
I want my half of the money.
I want everything good for the kids.

Bless my dear parents who are praying
that this is not going to happen.
Be pleased to redeem for me
what I sometimes regard as wasted years.
And may I make peace with this urge
to have someone, anyone, near.

Let me rise above the embarrassed eyes
that greet me each day at work.
Preserve forever the precious few
who know better than to give advice.
Make real every impulse to invite me to a meal.
And grant me the good sense
to buy an electric blanket
and stay away from bars.

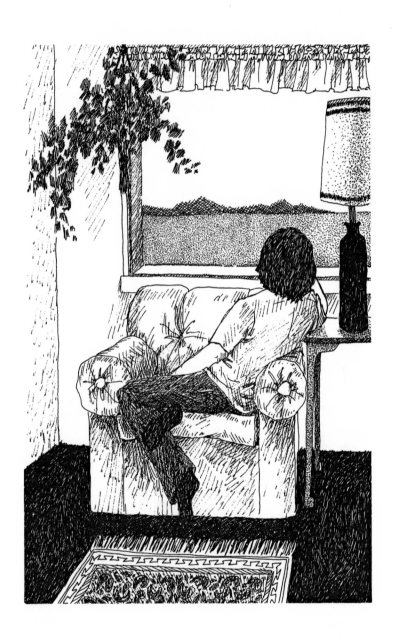

# PRAYER OUT OF BOREDOM

Lord of all my high resolve,
master of my purposes,
where are you now
when my thoughts drag me down
and my spirit growls within me?

Help me discover, out of all you have made,
the very thing that will unblock my stagnant self
and cause me to bubble and run free again.

Cross my path with your ministers
of variety and spice.
Clutter my way with colors and sounds.
Fill me with smells and flavors.
Prick my skin with perceptions I cannot avoid.

Trip me upon my lethargy.
Proclaim to me my laziness.
Rage against my hesitations,
and save me from this intimation of dying
that stalks me in the midst of life.

# PRAYER FOR A REDWOOD TREE

Its bark is soft and brownish red
and turns to dust in my fingers.
Its trunk is porous and musty.
Its leaves are small and spindly green,
its cones the size of a cherry.

God, how is it these fragile parts
come together in something so massive?
And why didn't the fires that charred it
burn it completely away?
And how shall we measure a life
that has lasted two thousand years?

I stand among ferns and mosses
and look up into a bramble of branches.
The tree towers above me.
I feel tiny beneath it.
I feel the deep chill of its shadow.

Thank you for those who spared this forest.
Thank you for the park it stands in.
Thank you for blue jays and squirrels
darting from limb to limb.

And thank you for the flicker of sunlight,
the slanting dust-filled beam,
the mushrooms poking through leaf mold,
this purple wild orchid
growing among huge gnarled roots
in a cranny away from the light.

# PRAYER OF THE ORDINARY

Now bless us who aspire to high places
but do our jobs in basements
where we stack the work of others
on vast well-ordered shelves.

Bless us who live in simple rooms
and like to walk and be alone
and take vacations but don't go far
and think a cup of coffee is a treat.

Bless us with our puppies and our warts
and our tendency to dream when wide awake.
Bless our sense of failure, if we sense it,
and bless our every unannounced success.

You who know the workings of our hearts
and the ordinary yearnings that we have,
surely know our need to feel uncommon,
if not to be considered quite unique.

So count again the sparrows as they fall,
the grains of sand along the dancing sea,
yes, the number of these precious hairs,
total them, if you please.

# PRAYER IN TRAFFIC

God of movement, beauty, and grace,
this is downright disgusting.
I watch the flashing taillights for a sign,
but when I change lanes,
the lane I left goes faster.
Why is everyone on this road moving except me?
Why does it seem like I've wasted my life
sitting alone in an idling car?

I'm tired of the radio.
I've had my fill of the rotten news.
I can see the weather for myself.
Everything imaginable has already been said
about last night's game.

Help me be tolerant of that guy in the helicopter
who flies above this freeway
and has the nerve to tell me it's a mess.
Deliver me from the urge to yell something stupid
at that noisy, smelly bus.
Ease my rage at cumbersome, big-shouldered cars
that crowd my two-door hatchback
and my jangled soul.

I've tried to learn a language as I commute,
and I couldn't order bread and cheese in Spain.
I've tried to notice my fellow travelers
and wish them well for the day,
but when I smile and wave they think I'm nuts.

There's no redeeming time in traffic, God,
so help me endure these moments of inching along
and cause me to recover from my bad attitude
within half an hour of arriving home.

# PRAYER FOR BLACKBERRIES

Why is it, O God of all delight,
that for every blackberry I pick
I get a scratch on my arm?
The berries are dark and luscious,
but the stickers are sharp and long.

The vines curl across the ground
from the lower reaches of the garden.
They climb the apple trees and birches.
They twist around the pillars of the porch.
The more I hack them, the faster they grow.

I can't work in the yard
without getting my trousers ripped.
Half my shirts are torn to shreds.
My socks are ragged and full of thorns.

If I had the power to do it,
I would condemn these vines to extinction.
I would visit them with terrible blight.
I would feed them to the eternal fire
and joyfully watch them burn.

But then in the height of summer
the berries turn black and sweet,
and I take buckets and bowls
and go forth again to pick them.
And we render them into homemade jam,
humming the hymn that says,
"Be still, my soul, thy best, thy heavenly friend,
Through thorny ways leads to a joyful end."

# PRAYER ON A VISIT TO A DYING FRIEND

Lifter of untold burdens,
I need you in these moments I am going through.
I must feel your presence as sureness and grit,
or flimsy feelings will fill my heart,
and I will add affliction to affliction
with my stammering words.
Amid your commitments in this hour,
be pleased to walk these fitful steps with me.

God, I want to rail against you
for this unfair visitation.
I want to curse you and crash the universe
in search of cures that you,
obviously, cannot provide.
I want to seal myself from your despicable doings
and shake my fist at heaven as I rage on.

Remind me of Jesus and how it must have been
for you to watch him suffer.
Remind me of hillsides in the spring,
of the stormy surf and pounding waves,
of raindrops as they splatter on a pond.

In the strength of our young bodies,
my friend and I planned and built new worlds.
Our voices rose within us and called forth
the hope and splendor in our souls.

Good God, I thank you for my friend,
and for these moments we will spend together.
Give me glimpses of those light-bathed worlds
we dreamed of years ago
even now as I enter this darkened room.

# PRAYER AT A SCHOOL BOARD MEETING

O God, if you preside over the councils of heaven,
how do you have time for anything else?
How do you manage to preserve your strength
in the midst of the eternal bickering?
How do you keep your sense of humor
among those who are ever so grave?

We have been here seven hours,
long enough, surely, to justify a sabbatical,
but the meeting goes on and on.

We have voted to expand the building,
and everyone agrees that's wise.
We have voted to let some teachers go,
because the budget is so tight.
We have cut the music program
and canceled the new books.
We're going to have a lovely campus
but not a school.

Forgive us for being blind to such incongruities.
Forgive us for accepting inadequate notions
of our fiscal responsibility.
Help us to work harder to find a better way.

The great mystery is that anything ever gets done.
And yet, somehow, children are being taught here,
the teachers have not given up,
young intelligence is being encouraged to grow,
ideas are leaping from mind to mind.

Thank you for the chance to say "aye"
to the spirit of education.
Thank you for every promise of fairness
we inadvertently fulfill.
And thank you, even,
for my well-meaning colleagues
who seem to speak ever so much
and say ever so little
and with whom I so seldom agree.

## PRAYER FOR PURPOSES

You who are working your purposes out,
I need you to help me with mine.
I need to know what lies behind
the steadily passing moments of my life.

My friend at the Chevrolet dealer's,
all he wants every morning
is to sell me a brand-new car.
How can it be so simple, God,
to know what is important about a day?

Help me look for questions as well as answers.
Help me feel the significance of the search.
Give me the courage to harbor ambiguity,
and grant me the wary openness
of those who earnestly seek.

Am I here to offer someone encouragement,
to help a child feel at home,
to think thoughts that have been thought before
and give them my own words?

The burden is on my shoulders, God,
the mist is in my eye.
I feel hemmed in by a thick stone wall
and can't seem to find the gate.

I ask for hints and guesses
of what a life is for.
I ask for current equivalents
of your clear voice from the sky.
I ask for a sense beyond sense
that I am finding my way.

# PRAYER FOR SAFE TRAVEL

God of distance and motion,
be with us now as we travel
this unfamiliar road.
Keep us alert as the sky darkens
and we are enveloped
by the massive shadows of the hills.

Give us starlight, streetlight, porchlight
for our guides.
Give us inner light.
Give us your own light.
Give us a road that takes us
where we want to go.

Lift our hearts beyond the loneliness
of these strange vistas.
Keep us curious and interested
in what we may find around the next bend.
And calm any anxiety
over how we will be received
when at last we arrive.

Include us now among your people
who were happy to call themselves travelers,
and grant us the sense that you move with us
everywhere we go.

# PRAYER IN THE MORNING

God of the timeless majesties,
for years I have looked upon you
as lofty and aloof
and yet this morning,
for no reason I can name,
I woke with my soul singing,
my heart refreshed,
and a hope for all your creatures
lodged within me.

This closeness is strange and frightening to me.
I am not accustomed to welcoming truth
into my neighborhood.
It is simpler to have you far away
from the ordinary doings of the world.

In fact, I am tempted at times
to accept a vision of myself
as a member of a hapless species
destined to prowl the universe on its own.

But now you are present in this new morning,
warm and comprehensible as a letter from home,
and whatever being I have
is alive and well and being born,
and my trembling sense of reality
steadies in this gentle, rising light.

# PRAYER ABOUT INCONSISTENCIES

Model of evenness and stability,
I waver in ways that would be humorous
if they weren't so deeply ingrained.

I set the alarm for six and get up at eight.
I take shortcuts when walking for exercise.
I sing hymns to the beauties of nature
and throw gum wrappers on the road.

I shudder to think of slaughtered animals
and ask for another helping of veal.
I worry about the greenhouse effect
and go kick tires on a shiny new car.
I speak of the sanctity of life
and, after three drinks, try to drive home.

I show up unprepared
and rail against incompetence
and don't notice anything odd
about this at all.

I long for singleness of heart
and persist in my duplicity.
It's as if my head is buried in the sand.

I do not ask you to change me.
I will never be constant or pure.
But if there's a way you can do it,
soften my impatience with others
and help me see what's really going on.

# PRAYER FOR A BEAT-UP CAR

O God, in whom nothing is wasted,
what happens to all this junk?
Along this road where I walk
there are cans and bottles and wrappers.
There are parts of bicycles, empty boxes,
and this beat-up car.

The car appeared a week ago,
abandoned where it finally stopped, I guess.
It was like a car I wanted once—
an old Volvo with a turtle body,
its little nose sticking out in front.
My, could those cars go.
The gearshift meshed with the motor
in a way that seemed organic.

Now this car sits beside the road,
every window broken, every fender bent.
Every part of it has been hit
with a rock or bullet or stick.

What makes us attack an abandoned car?
Why do we whack at whatever's there?
Why do we love destruction so much?

Creator and lover of matter's many forms,
renew our attitude toward forsaken things.
Instill in us respect for all that is.
And thank you for this fine old car,
for the journeys that it made,
for the people it brought together,
for its swiftness and precision when it was new.

# PRAYER IN APRIL

Now in the midst of April,
when the freeze gives way to glory,
and we are afraid the freeze will come again,
I try to pray, O God, and am soon overcome
by the delicate green of the grasses
and the struggle of blossoms in the wind.

I would rather praise you for eternal sameness
than for beauties that continually change.
I would rather complain about the oppressive winter
than give thanks for inspirations
that poke holes in the cynical dark.

But now there is whiteness and pinkness
and a softness that never was.
Now there is new life growing
around the fallen tree
and tender blades lapping against
the weather-shaped stones.

Our disciplined souls ask you
to protect us and save us, O God,
from indulgent springtime reveries.
Yes, we need your pull and prodding
on balmy days like this.

But still, in all wisdom and mercy,
allow our hearts some waywardness,
and grant us recurrent leisure
to enjoy your Aprils to the full.

# PRAYER FOR A VEGETABLE GARDEN

God of cucumbers, beans, and various squashes,
thank you for not making me a farmer.
With constant effort it's all I can do
to keep this little patch going.

Given the wild variety of bugs you created,
each reproducing according to its kind,
given the gophers, moles, and weeds,
given the hungry rabbits and voracious crows,
I barely get a taste of what I raise.

I don't know why I do this.
It's a summer habit, is what it is,
that got started years ago
when a friend looked me in the eye and said,
"Everyone's got to have a garden, you know."
It makes me think I'm accomplishing what I'm not.
Your sterner professors might call it idolatry.

But then I taste a tomato that tastes tomato.
I pick the ripened corn
and plop it into a pot of boiling water.
I slice the fresh zucchinis, snap the beans,
and sit down to a feast of flavors
that must be like the feasts in Eden
before the serpent said a word.

So I thank you for this garden, God,
and for the strength to tend it in my way,
and for my tiny harvest,
and for the tang and savor of each bite.

## PRAYER FOR GAZING

Seer of everything,
sometimes I like to stare at nothing.
I like to sit on the porch
and gaze at the landscape
and remember how, when I was a boy,
my father, the champion gazer, and I
would sit quietly for hours,
looking upon the lettuce fields
that stretched into the distance
behind our backyard.

Dad knew that to be a good gazer
you had to have an answer for those
who might ask what you were doing.
So, when Mom asked,
we said we were counting foxes.
And when she asked how many we had counted,
we said, "None, so far,"
and watched Mom roll her eyes.

There wasn't a fox within a hundred miles,
but if any had come by,
we surely would have counted them.

And so I gaze today and count the foxes
and remember everything
and nothing about my life.

And it feels so quiet and good
I think I'll keep on doing this for a time.
I think I'll keep on
remembering and forgetting all I am
and all I ever have been.

# PRAYER FOR JAZZ

Yes and oh, my goodness, God,
it must have been like this
on the thirteenth day of creation,
after you made the heavens and the earth,
after you rested,
and after the world had worked for a week
and come to that first real weekend,
you said, "Let there be jazz."
And there was jazz.

And it was very good,
just as this group I'm listening to right now
is so very good,
so sure of the beat,
so cool and swinging and hot.

"Yes," you said, "the people need jazz.
They need the mournful rhythms
of the field chants of the slaves.
They need the triumph song
when captives break their chains."

So you said, "Let there be pianos and saxophones
and trumpets and drums and flutes.
Let there be trombones and clarinets
and crashing cymbals and big bass viols.
Let there be guitars and vibraphones
and voices to sing lyrics and scat."

And you said, "Let there be Armstrong and Basie
and Charlie 'Bird' Parker and the Duke.
Let there be Goodman and Desmond
and Evans and Shelly and Getz.
Let there be Ella and Nat 'King' Cole
and Mel Torme and Red Norvo
and mellow Joe Williams and blue Lady Day
and all the sisters and brothers."

And you said, "Let the people listen,
let them clap their hands
and stomp their feet and shout.
Let them be refreshed
along their toilsome way."

You said, "Let there be jazz."
And there was jazz.
And it's so strong and beautiful
that even here in this smoky tavern
where this trio is rambling
through "Sweet Georgia Brown,"
we know it couldn't have happened
unless it came from you.

# PRAYER FOR WHALES

God of great movements and many migrations,
today we leave our human ventures
and gathered here to watch for whales.
On the cliff, a crackling fire
sends its smoke into the dripping sky.

Mossy boats, green and caked with barnacles,
ply the undulating waves beyond the point.
We set up our telescopes here on shore.

A spout! and every head swings that direction.
I look through the telescope
and my eye is met
by the wet gray skin of the whale.
I feel it stretched and massive
as it rises and falls back to the sea.

Nobody stirs. Nobody whispers.
The whale swims its long southward swim,
spouting, rising, diving,
calling out in a language, we are told,
that connects it to a lover
more than a thousand miles away.

And then the whale is gone.
The ocean swells against the cliff below us,
and our fire sputters and dies.

We put away our telescopes and pack our cars.
We drive toward our landlocked lives again.
And we wonder, O God, in the moment
before we snap on the radio and tune in the game,
if our needful, earnest human voices
are the only ones you hear and understand.

# PRAYER FOR A MOUNTAIN

Creator of purple and majesty,
my soul is lifted by this mountain.
Keep fresh this vision of loft and light
when I wander in shadowy valleys.
Remind me of these craggy summits
when I am too easily lulled
by the eternal sameness of the plains.

Speak to me always of sparkling snow
in the midst of summer,
of clouds clinging to peaks
like children to their mothers,
of waterfalls and evergreens
and everything that soars and climbs.

As I ponder my smallness against these cliffs,
help me to seek my place and no other.
May the deer and bear and crickets of this mountain
have nothing to fear from me.

O God, my lungs praise you for this air.
My limbs rejoice in these splashing waters.
My spirit leaps to the treetops
where the eagle spreads its wings.

Surely a world exists in what I now behold.
Surely the universe evolves
toward moments such as these.
Surely the human heart is most fully blessed
by what comes to it from on high.

All hail to you, O God, for this wild mountain
so far beyond our gentle hand-tamed hills.

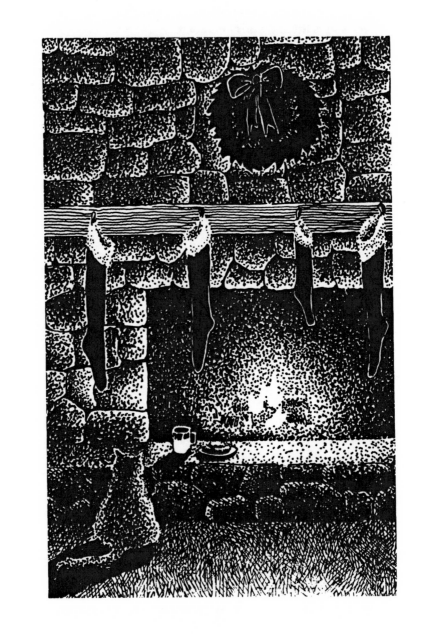

# PRAYER FOR A CHRISTMAS CAT

O God of this miraculous season,
please don't take offense,
but we have a cat here
who believes in Santa Claus,
a cat who came to us on Christmas years ago
and now has made us believers too.

We were going to call her Magus,
but that word was too hard,
so she became an "Angel" in our midst.
She never sings and seldom purrs,
but she enjoys her Christmases
as much as other angels ever do.

She sits by the glowing fire
every Christmas Eve and waits
for Santa to appear upon the hearth.
She's patient, still, and quiet
as the fire burns to coals,
as we put the kids and ourselves to bed.

In the morning Santa's cookie plate is empty,
his cup of cocoa too, and so we know
he's been to see us and left refreshed.

We ask your kindest blessing on this cat
who in her distinctive feline way
brings our house its annual mystery.
We thank you for the enchantment
in young and older eyes
as this story unfolds among us year by year.
And we praise you for the wonder
of your own Christmas story
from which our little family fable comes.

# PRAYER FOR A DREAM

Inhabiter of my nightly visions,
visitor in my slumber,
help me to know and trust my dreams.

I live in a time of vast separation
between the perceptions of waking light
and the pictures we see in our sleep.
I live in a time when everything happens
because of a first or second cause,
or because of a cause unknown.

But I have come upon mysteries
when the night was far spent
and my mind was free to wander
where I might encounter them.

Last night I saw a glistening pond,
a tree with strange and drooping leaves,
a place of shadows and light
like that of a photograph negative.
The sun or moon was high above the hills.
And two flying creatures flitted in the air
as if they had flitted there forever.
They made me feel I was not alone.
That's all I know about it.

Good God, my thanks to you
for every experience of your grace.
My thanks for the many ways
you make yourself known.
Speak to me as you will
and connect me ever more closely,
in my waking life, to whatever rises
from the rich shadows of sleep.

## PRAYER FOR A PRAYER

Knower of this, that, and the other,
I am becoming aware of things I wish weren't true—
    my lust and my duplicity,
    the desire to have more money,
    a craving to be well thought of far and near.
These small truths do not shake the universe, I know,
nor do they block your care for me.
They just make it hard for me to talk to you.

I would be silent. I would sulk and cringe.
I would head for beaches or for ball games
and forget your ways,
but nothing stays buried in my soul.
Nothing I wish to neglect recedes forever.

Can I rely on your knowing this,
to help me pray what I must pray?
And if you know what I will say,
why is it important for me to say it?
And what does it mean,
when I have always thought of you as far above me,
watching, smiling, frowning,
as I imagined Grandpa, who died and went to heaven,
that now I sense you someplace in my middle
and also all around me, clear and real as air?

God, to whom am I speaking?
And what does it mean to say a prayer?
And how does this fit
with the dance of light in treetops
or the wind howling in the dark?

I only know to pray, to ask, to cajole,
to badger the Almighty,
if almighty is what you are.
I only know to explain to you
what you already understand.

Father, Mother, Spirit, Child,
Force of Life and Press of World,
in your own way be known to me.
Bless those who pray with bones or feathers
or mystical cards or whirling wheels,
and be mindful of us
who are silent toward you most of the time
but who gratefully live
in the midst of all these prayers.

ROBERT JONES was born and raised in California, and studied at the University of California at Berkeley and Princeton Theological Seminary. He has served Presbyterian and Congregationalist churches in Pennsylvania, Kansas, and California. He now teaches preaching at Pacific School of Religion, writes a weekly column called "Keeping the Faith," and is finishing his doctorate at the Graduate Theological Union. His prayers, poems, and sermons have appeared in various journals, and his column has won several awards. The prayers collected in this volume have accumulated over many years.

GAY GUIDOTTI is also a native Californian. She began to draw at an early age, and her talent was well recognized by the time she reached high school. Her large mural of student life at El Molino High in Forestville, California, still graces the walls of one of the classrooms. Ms. Guidotti studied at the University of California at Santa Barbara, where she worked in the graphics department. She is now helping to run a water company and is raising two children. Like the prayers, her drawings have accumulated over the years, and now the prayers and pictures come together in this book.

CPSIA information can be obtained at www.ICGtesting.com
Printed in the USA
LVOW07s1826130515

438244LV00003BA/267/P

9 780664 253561